THE GIFT OF REMEMBRANCE

Ken Gire

Groove,
A little something' for all the big everything's you shared. ♥
With thanks & love in Jesus,
Claudia ☺

Daybreak Books

Zondervan Publishing House
Grand Rapids, Michigan

"In remembrance is the secret of redemption."

—Jewish proverb

In my scrapbook

of memories are many pictures that
are precious to me.

Three of them I will never forget.

I remember

a picture of Saturday nights and the
half-gallons of Mellorine ice cream
that Dad would buy,
three for a dollar.

One would go in the freezer.
    One would be divided between Mom and
    us three kids.
    The other he would spoon straight out
    of the carton for himself.

We kids would swirl ours with our spoons,
    making it soft and mooshy
    as we sat in front of the black-and-white TV,
    waiting for "Gunsmoke" to come on.

And when it did, we stood to face Matt Dillon,
    the marshall of Dodge City.

Standing in our terry-cloth robes,
    still dripping from our baths,
    we tried to outdraw the lawman
    who stood poised in the dusty street—
    his eyes steeled,
    his hand inches from the ivory on his
    six-shooter,
    waiting for us to make the first move.

Tension mounted.
The background music heightened,
then stopped.
We reached for our guns.
And in a split second
we were dead men.

Sprawled on the living room floor
in our terry-cloth robes.
Reduced to notches on the marshall's belt.

I remember
another picture.

A picture of Dad rubbing my legs when he
   tucked me in bed.
   "Growing pains," he called them.
   I remember those pains waking me up
   in the middle of the night.
   And however late,
   however often,
   he would come and rub the hurt away.
   How big his hands always seemed to me.
   How strong.

As he rubbed my legs, I could always beg a story out
   of him.
   A story about his early days as a coach.
   A story about the war.
   A story about when he was a boy, growing up in
   Kansas.

The stories about him growing up were my favorite.
   Stories of Halloween pranks
   and home remedies
   and the Depression.

Stories of his family on the front porch,
   huddled around the radio on the windowsill
   as they listened to "The Green Hornet"
   or "Lights Out."

Stories about *his* dad and mom, long since gone.
   Stories that brought them back to life
   so their grandson could wave to them,
   if only for a moment,
   if only from afar.

After he finished rubbing my legs,
we went through a little ritual
before he turned off the lights.

"I love you," he would say.
"I love you, too."
"How much?"
"Ten bags full," I answered, squeezing out a tired
little smile.
"That's all there is." And he tousled my hair.

Sometimes he would add,
"You'll never know how much I love you till
you have kids of your own."

That always puzzled me,
and I never knew quite how to respond.
Usually I just smiled and it ended there,
the mystery lying in my fallow mind
like a dormant seed
awaiting some springtime of understanding.

I remember

a third picture.

One Saturday when Dad was home—
   often he wasn't because he worked so much—
   I answered a knock on the door.

A handicapped boy,
   seventeenish,
   stood on the other side of the screen,
   selling socks.
   He introduced himself
   and went straight into his sales pitch.

His face contorted as he talked,
   most of the words coming out sideways-sounding.
   A flushed mingling of fear and sorrow
   came over me.
   With an awkward politeness I excused myself
   to get Dad.

He invited the boy in.
   I sat on the living room chair and just watched.
   The boy opened his briefcase, revealing
   an assortment of what I thought looked
   like "old-men's" socks. You know, the sheer,
   see-through kind that nobody wears
   anymore—except old men.

I didn't know much about money back then,
   other than how much you could get for cashing in
   Coke bottles littered along the roadside.
   All I knew was, we never seemed to have any.
   And what little we had never stretched far enough
   to cover the end of the month.
   So I listened
   to see how my dad would send the boy away.

But he didn't send him away.
   He listened to him with patience,
   spoke to him with kindness,
   treated him with respect.
   He examined the socks,
   and, to my round-eyed surprise,
   bought three pairs of those frightful things.
   Black, brown, and navy, if I remember right.

The boy shook my dad's hand and said good-bye.
   Then he shook mine,
   smiled,
   and stuttered something.
   I nodded as if I understood
   and smiled back.

A picture

of Saturday night fellowship
around half-gallon cartons of ice cream.

A picture of a tired father,
   rubbing away the leg pains of a growing son,
   adding a little story as salve.

A picture of a mentally disabled boy,
   treated with dignity and kindness.

Those were taken thirty years,
   twelve hundred miles,
   a wife and four kids ago.

But the pictures still live.

Dad never sat me down and told me,
   "Son, this is how you treat someone
   less fortunate than yourself,
   someone who's disabled or disadvantaged."
   He never told me that; he simply showed me—
   but with the purity of never knowing he did.

I found that when I wrote my first book,
   it was about a mentally disabled boy.
   When I did volunteer work,
   it was with the handicapped.
   And every time I encounter those who are
   in some way bent or broken,
   my heart softens.
   I send up a little prayer—
   that the load they carry
   may be made easier to bear,
   that they may be protected
   from the cruelties of this world,
   and that they may experience as much
   as they can of the goodness
   life has to offer.

And one more thing,
   I smile.

From what well are all these feelings drawn?
From the well of remembrance—
the remembrance of a picture
my dad showed me as a little boy.

Pictures.
They have a way of staying with you
and changing you.

Now I find that when I bring a treat home
for the kids,
it's usually ice cream.

When I tuck them in bed,
I tell them stories of when I was a boy.
I rub their legs.
I look at them tenderly.
I tell them I love them.
And before turning off the lights,
sometimes I say,
"You'll never know how much I love you
till you have kids of your own."

Now I know,
  because of them,
  how much my dad loved me.
  And someday,
  when they have kids of their own,
  they will know how much *their* dad loved them.

Pictures.
  They have a way of staying with you
  and changing you,
  far more profoundly and far more permanently
  than words ever could.

Maybe that's why the Word became flesh
  and dwelt among us.
  To give us pictures of God.
  To show us what brings a smile to His face,
  or a tear to His eye.
  To show us what He delights in,
  or what He detests.

The Word became flesh
  to make what was invisible, visible . . .
  to bring what was far, near . . .
  to show us God.

hat
ut

any of you who does not give up everything he has cannot be my disciple.

34"Salt is good, but if it loses its saltiness, how can it be made salty again? 35It is fit neither for the soil nor for the manure pile; it is thrown out.

"He who has ears to hear, let him hear."

The Parable of the Lost Sheep

15 Now the tax collectors and "sinners" were all gathering around to hear him. 2But the Pharisees and the teachers of the law muttered, "This man welcomes sinners and eats with them."

3Then Jesus told them this parable: 4"Suppose one of you has a hundred sheep and loses one of them. Does he not leave the nine-ty-nine in the open country and go after the lost sheep until he finds it? 5And when he finds it, he joyful-ly puts it on his shoulders 6and goes home. Then he calls his friends and neighbors together and says, 'Rejoice with me; I have found my lost sheep.' 7I tell you that in the same way there will be more rejoicing in heaven over one sinner who repents than over nine-ty-nine righteous persons who do not need to repent.

The Parable of the Lost Coin

8"Or suppose a woman has ten silver coins and loses one. Does she not light

earth about a day's wages.

she not light a lamp, sweep the house and search carefully until she finds it? 9And when she finds it, she calls her friends and neighbors together and says, 'Rejoice with me; I have found my lost coin.' 10In the same way, I tell you, there is rejoicing in the presence of the angels of God over one sinner who repents."

The Parable of the Lost Son

11Jesus continued: "There was a man who had two sons. 12The younger one said to his father, 'Father, give me my share of the es-tate.' So he divided his property between them.

13"Not long after that, the youn-ger son got together all he had, set off for a distant country and there squandered his wealth in wild liv-ing. 14After he had spent every-thing, there was a severe famine in that whole country, and he began to be in need. 15So he went and hired himself out to a citizen of that country, who sent him to his fields to feed pigs. 16He longed to fill his stomach with the pods that the pigs were eating, but no one gave him anything.

17"When he came to his senses, he said, 'How many of my father's hired men have food to spare, and here I am starving to death! 18I will set out and go back to my father and say to him: Father, I have sinned against heaven and against

"He who has seen Me has seen the Father."

The patriarchs and the prophets *told* us about God.
   Jesus *showed* Him to us.
   And when Jesus did tell us about the Father,
   He did so in the greatest short story ever written,
   the story of the Prodigal Son.

With His words, He brushes a picture—
   stripped of icons and haloes
   and baroque, ecclesiastical dross—
   a real picture,
   to show us all the heavenly Father is
   and all an earthly father is meant to be.

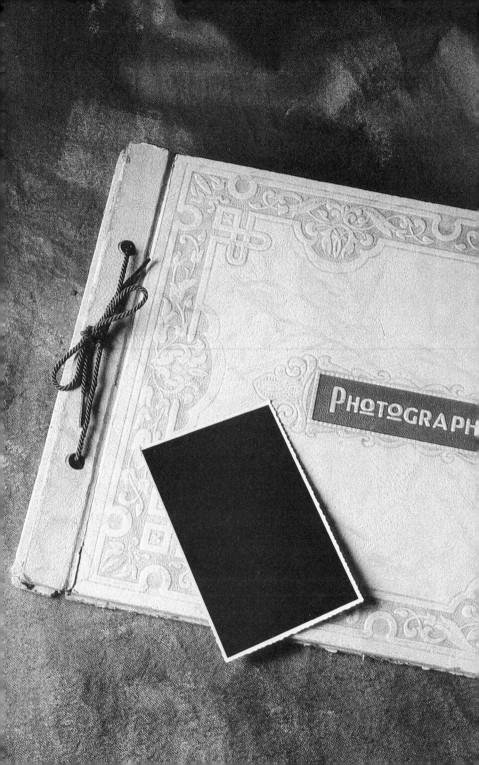

I have

one more picture that burns in my mind—
one I wish I didn't have.

LIGHTED DIAL

4:36

GENERAL ⊕ ELECTRIC

I remember

the digital clock reading 4:36
when the phone rang in the dark.
Whenever the phone rings at odd hours,
it can only be a wrong number or tragedy.
I hurried to the kitchen,
but just as I reached the phone,
whoever it was hung up.
Wrong number, I thought
as I returned to bed, relieved.

My head had just settled on the pillow,
when the phone rang again.
I walked down the dark hallway,
my feet growing heavier with each step.
I took a deep breath before picking up the receiver.
It was my brother.

"Ken? Rog."
The words lodged in his throat.
"Dad died."

He died quietly in his sleep. He was sixty-seven.

He had had his first, near-fatal heart attack
   when he was thirty-nine.

He had two open heart surgeries since then,
   hepatitis from a blood transfusion,
   diabetes,
   a gallbladder operation,
   cancer of the prostate gland,
   and numerous emergency visits to the hospital.

So, we were as prepared, I guess,
   as a family could be for news like this.

But you're never fully prepared
   for that final phone call.

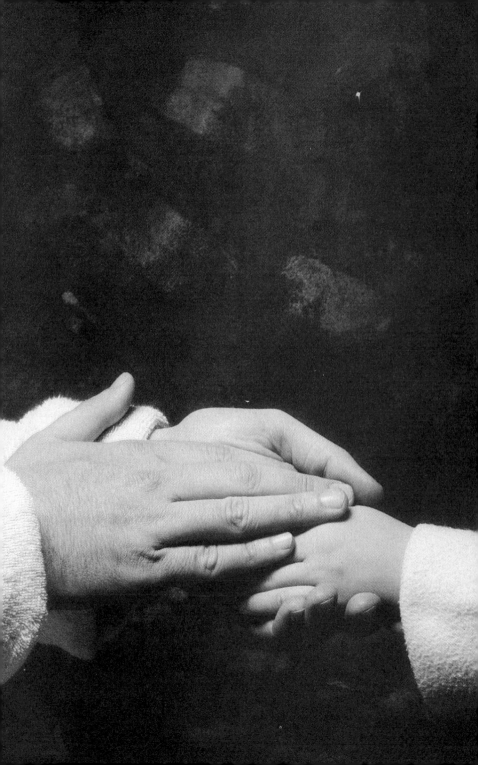

I waited
a couple of hours to tell the kids.

The hardest thing I've ever done was
   to wake them,
   gather them all together,
   and tell them their Grandpa was dead.

We all cried.

It started with me.
   Then the tears worked their way through the
   family, from oldest to youngest.

The funeral home was like a dream
  you pray to wake up from.

The body, once warm and flowing with life,
  lay cool and still
  in this somber, sequestered room.

He lay there like the shell a cicada leaves behind.

A shell where once lived someone you loved,
  someone who bought you ice cream,
  someone who told you stories,
  someone who rubbed your legs,
  someone who loved you.

A few days after the funeral,
  we flew back to California.

During that next year,
  those stacks of random pictures Dad left behind
  sorted themselves into neat, little piles
  and began mounting themselves in my mind.

The next summer I returned to Texas,
  to his grave.
  And as I sat there, those pictures returned to me.

How I missed him.
  How I longed to have him back,
  if only for an evening.
  And if an evening were granted,
  here is what we'd do:

We would walk down the lamplit streets, where,
  as a young boy,
  I would try to keep step with his stride.
  I would beg stories from him—
  stories about his coaching days,
  stories about the war,
  stories about when he was a boy.

And I would slip my little hand into his
   and feel secure
   in the dark and uncertain streets
   we walked together.

Then we would come home
   and share a half-gallon of ice cream.
   He would dish me out a bowl
   and spoon his out of the carton.

And then, I think, I would want to grow up again
   and talk with him as a man.

I would thank him for all the sacrifices he made.
   I would tell him I understand
   why he was gone so much,
   working so we could have life
   a little better than he had growing up.

I understand now, being a father myself,
   how hard it is to provide for a family,
   how hard it is not to be able to give your kids
   new clothes when school starts,
   piano lessons,
   a summer vacation.

I would

tell him how well the kids are growing up,
how they've changed since he last saw them.

I would tell him how they wept
when they heard the news of his death.

I would tell him how they missed his hugs
and the stories he would tell them
as they sat on his lap.

I would show him pictures of Judy and the kids.
(He was always so proud of them.)
And his smile would stretch across Texas,
from Tyler all the way to El Paso.

I would thank him for the memories.
I would tell him I miss him.
I would tell him I love him—*ten bags full.*
I would give him a hug.
And I would tell him good-bye.

As I sit here at the grave site,
   reflecting on the pictures left behind,
   it's important to note,
   not all of them were Norman Rockwells.

But love, it seems, really does have a way of
   covering a multitude of sins.

And by some mysterious mercy of God,
   some of the less pleasant, even painful,
   pictures start to fade away,
   leaving more room in the scrapbook
   for the really good ones.

The picture
before me now,
as I blink away the tears,
is the plain granite marker over his grave.
It has no epitaph.
He would have wanted it that way.

A warm tear slides down my cheek,
and I think to myself:
Tears from a son who loved him
is all the epitaph he ever would have wanted.

A shiver of my own mortality runs through me.

What pictures will *my* son remember
   when he comes to the plain granite marker
   over *his* father's grave?
   What will my daughters remember?
   Or my wife?

What pictures will be left behind
   for them to thumb through
   in the nostalgic, late afternoons
   of their lives?

Will the pictures strengthen them for the journey?
   Or send them hobbling through life, crippled.

I'm back home
with my family now, in California.

I've resolved to give fewer lectures,
 to send fewer platitudes rolling their way,
 to give less criticism,
 to offer fewer opinions.

After all, where does it say that a father
 has to voice an opinion on everything?
 Or even *have* an opinion on everything?

From now on, I'll give them pictures they can live by,
 pictures that can comfort them,
 encourage them,
 and keep them warm
 in my absence.

Because when I'm gone, there will only be silence.
 And memories.

Never again will I be able to say I'm sorry,
   I was wrong,
   forgive me.

Never again will I be able to tell them
   how much I love them,
   or how much they mean to me,
   or how proud I am of them.

Never again will I be able to tickle them,
   or smile into their eyes,
   or eat ice cream with them.

Never again will I be able to tuck them in,
   or tell them stories,
   or rub their legs.

Never again.

Of all
I could give
to make their lives a little fuller,
a little richer,
a little more prepared
for the journey ahead of them,
nothing compares to the gift of remembrance—
pictures that show they are special
and that they are loved.

Pictures that will be there
when I am not.

Pictures that have within them
a redemption all their own.

The Gift Of Remembrance
Copyright © 1990 by Ken Gire

Daybreak Books are published by
the Zondervan Publishing House
1415 Lake Drive, S.E.,
Grand Rapids, Michigan 49506

Library of Congress Cataloging in Publication Data
Gire, Ken.
    The Gift Of Remembrance / Ken Gire
        p. cm.
    ISBN 0-310-21780-6
    1. Fathers—Meditations. 2. Father and child—Meditations.
I. Title.
BV4846.G57 1990
242.6421—dc20   89-26038
                                                        CIP

"Published in association with Yates and Christian Communi-
cation Services, Orange, CA."

Printed in the United States of America

90 91 92 93 94 95 / DH / 6 5 4 3 2 1